Psalms
from the
Heartland

Psalms
from the
Heartland

Judy F. Hoff

Saint Mary's Press
Christian Brothers Publications
Winona, Minnesota

Printed on recycled paper
with soy-based ink

The scriptural text throughout this book is freely adapt-
ed. These adaptations are not to be interpreted or used as
official translations of the Scriptures.

The last two excerpts in Psalm 30 are from the song
"Though the Mountains May Fall," by Daniel L. Schutte.
Copyright © 1975 by Daniel L. Schutte and New Dawn
Music, 5536 NE Hassalo, Portland, OR 97213. All rights
reserved. Used with permission.

Psalm 62, "First Americans," is based on an article enti-
tled "Young Sioux Speaks Out," by Wipe Out [pseud.],
Woyakapi, Saint Francis High School, Saint Francis, SD.
Used with permission.

The publishing team included Carl Koch, FSC, devel-
opment editor; Cheryl Drivdahl, copy editor; Amy
Schlumpf Manion, production editor and typesetter;
inside illustrations by Elaine Kohner; cover illustration by
Charles Capek; cover design by McCormick Creative; pre-
press, printing, and binding by the graphics division of
Saint Mary's Press.

Printed in the United States of America

Printing: 6 5 4 3 2 1

Year: 1999 98 97 96 95 94 93

ISBN 0-88489-295-6

Thanks
to my family and friends
  for their love and support,
to the professionals
  who gave advice and encouragement,
to those who shared
  their time and thoughts in interviews,
to Lois Stewart,
  who understood what my heart needed to say.

Contents

Preface

The Origins of
Psalms from the Heartland

I was standing at the kitchen sink, washing dishes, thinking and praying about a family that were losing their land in a foreclosure. As I pondered the deep sorrow of the family about to be deprived of their livelihood and way of life, a voice urged me, "Write it down."

So I sat at the dining table, trying to write the story of this family. I knew their sadness and what laments they would send to God. When I turned to the Psalms for inspiration, I knew they were what I needed to pray about the heartland. Over the years, I had heard many woeful and wonderful tales, and I hoped that in praying the stories, I would heal some of the wounds and celebrate some of the wonders. At the time, I did not dream that my prayers would take form in a book. I just needed to tell God what was on my mind and in my heart.

These psalms from the heartland are shaped from many stories I have heard of wounded families and divided rural communities, of family farms being lost and small-town businesses closing, of unkind words and destructive actions between neighbors, of injustices and lack of cooperation by institutions, and of church members failing to love one another. But they are also psalms of people tempered and strengthened, of conflicts resolved and fair treatment given, of sensitive stewardship and generosity of spirit, of compassion and concern, and of laughter, love, and thanksgiving.

When I prayed the Psalms, a story would sometimes come to mind. At other times, I would reach out to a biblical psalm for an understanding of a story in my heart.

The biblical psalms show all the emotions that flow within us if we are humble enough to admit them. Reading the biblical psalms is like listening to an intense, honest, emotional conversation between two people who are not afraid to be themselves with each other, even in their deepest fear and anger. I hope these psalms from the heartland are as honest.

I also wanted to be just. So I composed psalms from interviews with people who sit across the desk from ranchers and farmers: loan officers, attorneys, sheriffs, and businesspeople. For instance, Psalm 18, "Serving Papers," takes the perspective of a deputy sheriff having to deliver legal papers. Psalms about family life and love of the land, relationships and behavior, and praise of God are interspersed among the lamentations. Good times and bad times, beautiful sunrises and sad finales mix in our life. At least, they have in mine.

I was born in a small North Dakota town. Growing up there, I helped in my parents' store and attended school; then I taught, married Jim, raised nine children, and lived and worked on and off our river ranch in the southwestern part of the state. Despite difficulties, my life has been blessed with a sure knowledge that I am loved by family, friends, my church community, and my creator God. So, besides being a story of life in the heartland, this book is also an act of thanksgiving, faith, hope, and love.

I hope these psalms bring healing too. Healing begins when we better understand one another and when we take the time to pray about our experiences. Over time, we may forgive ourselves and other people, let go of fear, and grow in trust.

Finally, I also hope these psalms touch readers who know little about rural America and allow them a glimpse of our way of life. In any case, many of these psalms reflect universal human experiences.

Praying Psalms

As you pray these psalms, allow yourself to feel what each psalm says. When a psalm laments the loss of a farm, lament your own loss of an important part of your life. When a psalm praises God for a rich harvest or a magnificent sunset, praise God for the natural blessings around you, whether you live on a farm in Virginia or you live in the heart of San Francisco. See the hawks overhead and the miles of Dakota sky as symbols of all God's creation, all that nourishes your body, spirit, and mind. And when a psalm releases anger, let your own anger be purged as you express yourself in its words. The spirit of praying biblical psalms and these psalms from the heartland should be a spirit of absolute honesty with a loving God who knows our heart and mind.

These psalms may be incorporated into longer prayer services by adding hymns, biblical passages, and time for shared reflections. Or use a single psalm as the subject of meditation or journal writing. Let the psalm inspire praying about your experience.

I thank again my loved ones and all the people whose stories went into these prayers. May God be with you.

JUDY HOFF
Carson, North Dakota

1. True Happiness

Blessed are they who turn away
from the advice of evil people,
who turn away
from the example of sinners.

(Psalm 1:1)

Are those who prey on others
the most evil of people?
They seek out the vulnerable,
the hurt, the old, the angry.
They feed on the anguish of those
who are already in pain.
They take advantage of people
for their own gain.
But their gain is like chaff;
it will be blown away in the wind.
People who choose instead to be upright
will find joy in obeying God's law.
They will be truthful and trustworthy,
helpful, compassionate, and caring.
They will bear good fruit for all to see;
they will be an example for many.
They will be people of justice and love.
They will walk humbly with their God.

God guides and protects the way of the just,
but evil ones are on their way to doom.

(Psalm 1:6)

2. Heal Me, God

Answer me when I call, O God.
You have always helped me when I had troubles.
You are a gracious God;
hear my prayer.

(Psalm 4:1)

O God, I can only pray at home.
I am not comfortable in our church.
When I look up and see him seated across from me,
I have such sadness in my heart that I can't pray.
I don't want this anger and hurt inside me.
It's over and done;
our land is theirs now.
I come to my church
to hear the words and songs that will comfort me.

I leave upset
because he was there.
So I read your word at home;
your holy book is my friend.
I sing songs of praise and thanksgiving
as I go about my day.
In the evening, I pray for healing,
so I can again go to my church
and feel at home.

> I lie down in peace, and sleep
> in the safety and comfort of God.

(Psalm 4:8)

3. Lead Me

> Listen to my prayer, O God,
> and hear my cry for help.

(Psalm 5:1–2)

It's late.
I stayed up to watch a spy thriller on television.
It wasn't very good, but that doesn't matter.
I wouldn't have slept anyway.
Today, my lender asked me to spy on my neighbor,
to watch where and when he moves cattle,
to note if there are other brands in his herd.
My lenders have security in my assets.
They have no claim on my soul!
How could one of them have asked this of me?
I wonder if others are spying too.
There's tension among neighbors.
Our community is splitting apart.
This kind of behavior only furthers the breakdown.
Turn to me, O God, and relieve me of my worries.

Teach me to live according to your truth,
for you are my God.
At least you I can trust.

Lead me, O God, to do your will;
show me the correct path to follow.
You are not pleased with wrongdoing;
nor do you allow evil in your sight.

(Psalm 5:8,4)

4. *Hear My Weeping*

Have pity on me, God,
for I am worn out—
exhausted—
and filled with fear.
How long, God, until you hear me?

(Psalm 6:2–3)

She is our beautiful daughter;
she made our family complete.
But now, she is ill,
and pain racks her body.
Our family surround and comfort her;
we cry out to God in prayer.
Come and save her, God;
in your mercy, rescue her.
I am worn out with grief;
my pillow is wet with tears.
I can hardly see those around me;
my eyes are swollen from weeping.

O God, hear my weeping!
Listen to our cries.
Accept our prayers, and answer us.

(Psalm 6:8–9)

5. *The Dignity of People*

O God, our God,
your majesty fills all the earth.
The praise of your people reaches the heavens.
I behold your creation and wonder:
what is humanity, that you think of us,
that you should regard us?
You have made us but a little lower than yourself,
crowning us with honor,
giving us authority over the work of your hands.

(Psalm 8:1–6)

The power you give us is overwhelming!
But are we good stewards?
Or does our comfort, our convenience,
our apathy, our greed interfere?
Do we practice dominion over other people
by their ethnicity, their socioeconomic status,
their education, their work, their ability?
Are we good stewards of the land, air, water,
and all that lives there?
Do we treat properly the animals
entrusted to our care?
You set us above all other earthly creatures, O God,
when you gave us a conscience
to choose right or wrong.
You really took a chance, God,
when you gave us free will.

God looked at everything created
and was very pleased.
O great God, are you still pleased?
Is your greatness seen in all the world?

(Genesis 1:31)

6. *Friends and Neighbors*

God is a refuge for those who are oppressed,
a safe place for those who are troubled.
All who know you, God,
trust you to help them.
You do not forsake anyone who comes to you.

(Psalm 9:9–10)

How wonderful it is to have good friends!
Their home is our safe house.
Their hearts are our refuge.
We go to them just as we go to you, God.
They lessen our fears with kind words.
Their happiness increases our joy.
They don't close the door
to those who need shelter,
but welcome them with warmth and laughter.
With them, we find comfort and rest.
We entrust our problems
to their quiet understanding,
allowing their wisdom to be our light.
Their honesty calls us to goodness.
Holy Friend, they know
they are only your servants.
They do not judge or question our ways,
but gently lead us on your paths.
The love they have for you, O God,
is manifested in the love they have for us.
We sing with joy for your people!

I will praise you, God, with all my heart.
I will be glad and extol your wonderful deeds.
I will sing in joyful praise to you, almighty God.

(Psalm 9:1–2)

7. Their Livelihood

O God, why are you so far away?
Why do you hide yourself from those in need?

(Psalm 10:1)

I've worked so hard as an attorney, God,
doing everything I can.
Still, I feel an anxiety, a concern for my clients.
O God, the hardest thing about this work
is knowing that this is not just a case.
This time, I'm dealing with their livelihood.
They may lose their farm.
My clients are just like everyone else.
They vary in talent or ability.
Some decisions, based on best knowledge,
proved wrong.
Whether circumstances or poor judgment
caused their trouble,
it doesn't matter.
What's important to me now is to help them.
My work will affect their life, their family;
the farm is their heritage, their home.
Help me, my God, to serve my clients well.

You do see, God;
you take notice of trouble and grief.
You hear the prayers of the humble.
You strengthen our heart.

(Psalm 10:14–17)

8. Trust

Help us, God!
Are there no good people left?
The words of others lack sincerity;
we cannot depend on them.

(Psalm 12:1–2)

We made a change again in the repayment date,
and we reached a new agreement.
It was verbal,
and I am anxious
until the letter of confirmation comes.
I don't rely on the words from his mouth.
Only when I see them on paper will I relax.
This feeling is like a weight dragging me down.
Then I realize what the real hurt is.
I need to trust people!
I have always believed
in the goodness of your people, my God.
How can I ask him to believe me,
if I do not believe him?
I may be harmed by this new openness,
but it cannot be as harmful as what happens to me
when I am so suspicious.

Your words, O God, can always be trusted.
They are as genuine
as silver smelted in the furnace,
seven times refined.

(Psalm 12:6)

9. How Long, God, How Long?

Will you forget me forever?
How much longer
will you hide your face from me?
How long will my enemies harm me?

(Psalm 13:1–2)

I can hardly pray anymore;
my prayers have become begging.
I have no pride in myself;
I am nothing.
My enemies will take away my land.
They fight over my possessions.
My neighbors mock me and speak ill of me.
They take delight in my fall.
My children are confused.
They knew a strong father;
now they are unhappy and bewildered;
they reject me in my weakness.
My wife scorns me and turns away.
Where is my faithful support?
I cannot live this way any longer;
the grief and hurt overwhelm me.
There is nothing I can change;
I cannot make life better.
Only death will bring release;
death will take away the pain.

You give me sorrow
and fill my heart with grief.

(Psalm 13:2)

10. Words

Who may enter your temple, O God?
A person who obeys you always
and does what is just,
who speaks in truth and sincerity.
One who does not speak or listen to slander,
harm a friend,
or condemn a neighbor.

(Psalm 15:1–3)

A good friend corrects and rebukes in kindness,
but will not speak of your sin to others.
Yet, when some people gather together,
their gossip becomes like a feast.
They delight in spreading rumors
and slandering those around them.
They choose to speak in half-truths;
innuendos and insinuations are their joy.
Like feathers blowing in our north winds,
their words cannot be gathered up.
By the evil of their words,
they seek to destroy others.
By their lack of truth and sincerity,
they destroy themselves.

O God, set a sentry at my mouth
and a guard at the door of my lips.

(Psalm 141:3)

11. Settlers

Keep me safe;
O God, I put my trust in you.
My future rests in you alone.
God is at my right hand;
I am secure.

(Psalm 16:1–9)

The people who settled
the fertile plains of the Dakotas
came from many countries.
Farmers, merchants, and tradespeople
traveled across the ocean to an unknown land.
Most came with few material possessions.
They usually settled with "their own kind"—
people of their culture and religion.
They built homes, stores, schools, and churches—
the heart of their community.
The legacy they gave us
was the values they lived.
They had a deep faith in God,
a strong commitment to family,
a willingness to work hard,
patient endurance,
and a love of life.
That is what lives on in us!

I am thankful and glad and secure.
You make known to me the path of life.
In your presence, I am filled with joy!

(Psalm 16:9–11)

12. God's Hand Protects

God is my protector,
in whom I take refuge.
My God is my stronghold,
defending me and keeping me safe.

(Psalm 18:2)

I watch my rancher husband
come in from the storm.
He carries a newborn calf, struggling for life.
I witness his strength and tenderness
as he places the calf in warm water.
In minutes, heat courses
throughout the newborn body.
And then, the calf fights the water that saved him
and the hands that protected him.
How much like the foolish calf we are, good God.

In our despair, we cry to you for help,
and you lift us up.
You give us strength to overcome our troubles.
Your power flows through us.
But then, we each stand and say, "I can do this,"
and we turn away from the God who saved us.
In our foolishness, we think
we are power and strength.
O God, help us to know that
we are nothing without you.

> God alone is our strength,
> protecting and caring for us.

(Psalm 18:31–32)

13. *The Minister*

> May God answer you in your distress.
> May the God of Jacob protect you
> and send help from the temple
> and give you aid.

(Psalm 20:1–2)

Merciful God, how can this be happening?
They are my people.
Only when I saw the auction posters
did I know of their troubles.
I spoke to their friend in our church
and heard of their struggles.
How can I minister to them
when I do not know their pain?
O God, when someone dies, I am called;
I console the family.
When someone is very sick, I am summoned:
"Remember her in prayer."

Have I failed by not seeing their hurt?
Did I miss the signs?
When often they weren't in church,
did I visit and ask why?
The hour is late, but not too late.
I'll go to them now.
Losing a farm is often like a death.
Let me minister to them.
Our church members will stand with them;
we'll help and support them.
God, help my people know that I am here for them.
I am their shepherd.

> We trust in your holy name, O God.
> Answer us when we call.

(Psalm 20:9)

14. *His Friend*

> He is glad, O God,
> because you give him strength.
> He rejoices because of your help.
> You have granted his heart's desire.

(Psalm 21:1–2)

I can't count the nights of crying,
the nights of loneliness.
I waited for him to come home,
yet dreaded his return.
Alcohol was his demon,
he embraced it as his friend;
it mastered his soul.
I hated it when he was drinking;
sometimes,
I hated him.

His promises,
like our dreams,
were empty and broken.
In his sorrow, we prayed together;
we implored God for help.
That help came to us in his friend;
he understood our pain.
He told us what we had to do.
He encouraged us to do it.
It has been such a long struggle.
We cried; we prayed; we held each other.
Gentle-yet-firm hands reached out to us.
Listening hearts helped us heal.
Thank you, God, for sending your people;
they've lifted us out of hell.

> He asked for life, and you gave it.
> You bless him forever.
> In your presence, he is filled with joy.

(Psalm 21:4–6)

15. A Cry for Help

> My God, my God,
> why have you abandoned me?
> I cry out to you; you do not hear.
> Day and night, I ask for your help,
> but it does not come.

(Psalm 22:1–2)

This was my father's land.
As a child, I watched him till the soil
and plant the trees.
I saw my children grow and mature on this land,
as I tried to guide them in your ways.

Now, you are allowing my enemies to surround me
and take that for which I have labored.
They divide our possessions among them.
Trouble is all around,
and no one can help us.
My strength is gone,
gone like water spilled on parched ground.

You are my God!
I have always depended on you.
Don't stay away from me.

(Psalm 22:10–11)

16. *My Cup Is Full*

Gentle God, you are my shepherd.
I shall not want.
You lead me on the right path.
You prepare a table before me;
I am the honored guest.
My cup is overflowing.

(Psalm 23:1–5)

A long time ago,
circumstances caused us to move
from the ranch into town.
Life was different.
School was close to the back door.
Our children had playmates
other than sisters and brothers.
But with their father working out on the ranch
and us in town,
we didn't have much time with him.
One stormy winter,
the roads were impassable.
We hadn't seen Dad for days.
He phoned and told us
he was coming for Sunday dinner—
on horseback.
He would have to cross the frozen river
and travel eight miles through snowbanks,
but he was coming!
Everyone was excited.
All put on their best dress
or nicest shirt.
Curls and ribbons,
boots and belts were in place.
The finest dishes and best cloth were on the table,
and Dad's favorite meal was on the stove.
The journey proved long and cold,
but the joy and delight of his wife and children
warmed him and made it worthwhile.
It was a good day.
In the dark stillness of early morning,
secure in the love of his family,
he returned to the ranch and the livestock.

Though I go through the darkness,
I have no fear,
for you are with me.
Your goodness and kindness will follow me
all my life.

(Psalm 23:4–6)

17. *We Belong to God*

The earth is God's!
All who live on the earth
belong to God.

(Psalm 24:1)

The brokenhearted and the menders belong to God.
The hurting and the healers belong to God.
The sorrowful and the comforters belong to God.
The troubled and the counselors belong to God.
The despairing and the hopeful belong to God.
The oppressed and the liberators belong to God.
The angry and the peacemakers belong to God.
The sinners and the confessors belong to God.
The uneducated and the teachers belong to God.
The sick and the nurses belong to God.
The hungry and the farmers belong to God.

Such are the people who come to God,
who seek the face of God.

(Psalm 24:6)

18. Serving Papers

Declare that I am innocent, O God,
because I follow your laws.
I trust in you completely.

(Psalm 26:1)

It's a sad job, God,
serving papers on a farmer,
on a businessperson,
or at someone's home.
I know this could be the start
of tougher times ahead.
My God, these are good people;
some are friends.
I try to treat them with consideration and respect.
And still, God, I can become
the target of their pain.
I'm there,
so they often take their anger out on me.
Lots of folks are struggling;
it affects all of us.
Some days, when I take off my uniform and badge,
I go to my neighbors to help them with their work.
I sense a lack of trust;
I feel their suspicion
that I'm just a tool of the lending agencies.
Sometimes, papers are served
through certified mail.
People might put them aside,
not knowing what to do.
At least, when I go out, I'll ask if they understand.
I can tell them to get some help, some counsel.
Maybe they can talk to me as a neighbor
or even a friend.

Some people wonder how I can do this "dirty
  work."
I tell myself, "Better me than someone who doesn't
  care."
I'd like to wash my hands of it and see the law
  changed.
Mostly, I pray for a good economy, for people to
  cooperate.
Only then will there be fewer papers for anyone to
  serve.

  Your kindness goes before me.
  Your faithfulness leads me.

                                        (Psalm 26:3)

19. *Caring*

  God is my light and my salvation.
  Whom shall I fear?
  God is my protector.
  Of whom shall I be afraid?

                                        (Psalm 27:1)

We read it in the paper.
Our neighbor's land is for sale,
for sale by the creditor.
We didn't know their troubles were so serious.
We phone and offer our help.
During the night, I can't sleep;
my heart is pounding.
I fear for them;
I fear getting mixed up in this.
I wonder how being part of it might affect us.
I wonder how I'll feel
meeting with some of the people involved.

I pray for the light and strength to know what to do
and the courage to do it.
We go to our friends;
we listen.
We go through records with them.
We sit in mediation with them.
We visit their creditors with them.
Finally, a settlement is reached.
The land sale is stopped.
We're glad for them and hopeful for their future.
That night, I thank God,
and sleep restfully.

> Trust in God.
> Have courage in your heart.
> Trust in God.

(Psalm 27:14)

20. *Tears in the Night;*
Joy in the Morning

> I cried to you, my God,
> and you healed me.
> Sing to God, all faithful people.

(Psalm 30:2–4)

There was a time when I thought
I would never laugh again.
Sorrow had filled my heart for so long;
night and day,
I called out to you, God.
It seemed my prayers were useless.
You did not hear me.
I cried out to you again;
my prayers were left unanswered.

Now I know joy in my morning,
joy in this new life.
You hear my prayer;
you strengthen and heal me;
I meet the new day.
You have taken away my sadness
and filled me with joy.
My sorrow has been changed
into a song of gladness.

I sing of your glory;
I will not be silent.
O God, my God,
I will thank you forever.

(Psalm 30:12)

21. *Forgiveness*

Happy the one whose sins are forgiven,
whose wrongs are pardoned.
Happy the one in whom there is no deceit.

(Psalm 32:1–2)

They have had some of their debt forgiven, God.
It's so unfair!
They drive a new truck,
but we can barely afford to repair our old one.
We worked hard to pay our bills,
and they wasted what they got.
Now, ashamed, I lie in the quiet of the night
and remember the debts
you have forgiven me, my God.
You have written off all my wrongs
and wiped away my offenses.
And I recall how often
I waste what you have given me, my God.
Some friends had a paper listing
the debts people in the county have had forgiven.
O loving God, may there never be a list
of what each of us has had forgiven by you.

If you, O God, kept a record of our sins,
who could stand?
But you are a forgiving God.
Teach me the way I should go,
instruct and advise me.
Let me obey you and shout for joy.

(Psalm 130:3–4; 32:8–11)

22. Mountains and Valleys

By God's command, the heavens were created,
the sun, moon, and stars.
By God's word, the world was created.

(Psalm 33:6–9)

We often use your creation to describe our life,
O God.
We talk of the difficult times as valleys and
mountains.
People have a mountain
of overwhelming problems and pain in their life.
They cry out that they cannot make the climb;
they need help.
I ask you, "Please, God, take away this valley in my
life."
But you, God, don't make the valley less wide or
less deep.
Instead, you walk beside me and comfort me.
I walk on in faith and in trust.
Friends and family come to lighten the load.
They give me hope.
Have you noticed the change,
defined or subtle,
in people who have climbed a mountain
or walked a valley?
Some draw closer to their God.
Maybe they take a deeper appreciation
of family and friends.
Perhaps they have courage and power
to use the gifts God had already given them.
You did not promise, creator God,
that life would be a smooth, level plain.
Instead, you promised always to be with us.
All my thanks to you, the source of true mercy.

God watches over those
who show reverence and trust.
My soul looks with hope to God,
my protector and help.

(Psalm 33:18–20)

23. *Fear and Prayer*

I will thank God at all times.
Let those who are discouraged
listen and be glad.
We will praise God together.

(Psalm 34:1–3)

The bank had been closed!
Personnel from the FDIC
had invaded their small town.
Emotions ran high, and rumors abounded.
Families who had banked there for generations
were stunned.
Fear gripped many farmers and ranchers.
Drought
plus low prices
had put them in the "troubled loan" category.
Businesses dependent on agriculture
were concerned.
With fear came confusion and anger.
The young pastor often led his congregation
in prayer for various groups of people.
Audible sighs coursed through the church
when he asked his people
to pray for the people from the FDIC.
They prayed with him for those they feared.
They came and listened
and learned one way to have reverence for God.

They prayed for God's people,
even those who might seem to be enemies.

> I prayed to God and was answered.
> I was freed from my fears.
> Our God is near to those who feel oppressed,
> strengthening their spirits with hope.

(Psalm 34:4–18)

24. *God Is Good!*

> Your kindness, O God, reaches to the heavens;
> your faithfulness stretches to the skies.
> Your justice is like the highest mountain,
> your wise decisions like the greatest depths.

(Psalm 36:5–6)

People and animals rest in your care.
Your love, our Creator, is infinitely precious.
You are the source of all life and light;
in your light, we see light.
I call to you, God,
the most high God, who gives bountifully to me.
My heart stands steadfast in you, O God;
I sing your praises.
I will thank you always among friends and enemies;
I will make happy music for you, bountiful God.

> Be exalted, O God, in the highest heavens;
> show your glory over all the earth.

(Psalm 57:5)

25. *A Way of Life*

> Trust in God and do good;
> live in the land and be safe.
> Commit your ways to God,
> and you will be granted your heart's desire.
>
> (Psalm 37:3–4)

They say we should stop thinking of ranching
as a way of life;
it's only a business.
Like other businesspeople,
we plan, work, buy, sell, assess,
do endless paperwork,
and make hard choices.
Unlike most businesspeople,
we cannot close the doors and go home.
Our ranch is home.
In our business,
most of the family are part of the team.
Together, we meet the challenges;
together, we reap the rewards.
Based on skills and time,
a husband and wife
share the work and responsibility.
According to age and ability,
a child pitches in and gives a hand.
A fourteen-year-old moves cattle along the river for
    six weeks.
An eight-year-old saddles her horse to help move
    the herd.
A sixteen-year-old prepares the paperwork for a
    loan.
A twelve-year-old assists with a difficult birth.
Nature affects many businesses,
but none year-round as much as a ranch.

We witness the miracles of nature;
we also feel its power.
When a grade school class wrote
about the effects of a severe spring storm,
the town kids wrote
of inconvenience and adventure.
The country kids wrote
of their family's endless hours of work
to care for their livestock in the raging storm.
Ranching is like weaving a tapestry.
Through the beautiful colors of the seasons
are woven our work,
our family,
our faith in God,
our values, finances, community living, school,
friends, activities, and socializing.
We cannot separate our job from our life;
the threads do not pull apart.

God sees those who are faithful and just;
the land will be theirs forever.

(Psalm 37:28–29)

26. My Life

O God, make known to me
the measure of my days.
Is my life just a vanity?
I am no more than a puff of wind,
no more than a shadow.

(Psalm 39:4–6)

My life is minutes
compared with the years people have walked on
this earth.

Like a puff of wind
compared with the length and scope of God's
      eternity.
I am only a guest for a little while
before I go away and am no more.
Teach me how short my life is,
so that I may become wise, Spirit of God.
The riches of the world crumble;
they cannot be kept at death.
Love lasts forever.
Teach me to love faithfully.
To love God and to love all people.
To reach out to others and not count the cost.
To lift people up and tear walls down.
To forgive and care, not judge and hate.
To be filled with God's mercy and law,
and empty of selfishness and injustice.

> Fill us, O God, each morning with your kindness,
> so that we may sing in joy
> and be glad all our days.

(Psalm 90:14)

27. Here I Am

> O God, you do not want sacrifices and burnt
>   offerings.
> Your instructions to me are written in the book
>   of law.
> You have given me ears to hear you,
> and I answer, "Here I am."

(Psalm 40:6–7)

A semi jackknifed with a load of lambs.
It would take a lot of horsepower to lift it.
Each came with a tractor; "Here I am."
He had died suddenly, with little warning.
Her heart was breaking; tears welled.
A friend offered a shoulder; "Here I am."
They needed to round up and sort cattle.
An extra horse and rider would be a help.
They phoned; he answered, "Here I am."
Their tractor was mired down and sinking.
They asked for his aid and all-wheel drive.
He heard their need and came; "Here I am."
Upset, they couldn't understand each other.
A friend can often see both points of view.
Over coffee, he helped them see; "Here I am."
His illness came at a bad time.
The crops were ready to be harvested.
Neighbors gathered to reap; "Here I am."
They come from shops, stores, and jobs,
into an ambulance or out to a fire.
Thank God, volunteers say, "Here I am."
The knowledge of God's love for all of us
is a treasure to be shared with others.
They gather youth, teaching them; "Here I am."
He wanted to get away for a few days of rest.
He had to start pasture wells every day.
A neighbor kid smiled and said, "Here I am."
She was being taunted by other students.
Her clothes weren't as good as theirs.
Someone put a hand on her arm; "Here I am."

    I love to do your will, my God!
    Your law is written in my heart.

(Psalm 40:8)

28. Come to the Well

As a deer longs for the brook of cool water,
So I long for you, O God.
My soul thirsts for you, living God.

(Psalm 42:1–2)

As we drive through a different countryside,
we see wells next to grain fields and in pastures.
They pump oil from the richness of the earth.
I say, "Why them; why not me?
Oh, that I could have such riches."
But then, I do have such riches!
I have a well of God's grace,
deep and ever flowing.
I draw from it when I am sad or troubled.
I fill myself and increase my joy.
It is always enough!

How precious and everlasting
is the love of the living God!
May I always thirst for it.

(Psalm 42:11)

29. Gifts

Beautiful thoughts fill my heart,
as I compose this poem for my Creator.
My tongue is filled with words,
like the pen of a good writer.

(Psalm 45:1)

A song of valleys and faith, a quilt sewed with love.
Our talents and abilities are gifts from God's grace.
A doctor's skilled hands, a teacher's wisdom shared,
a neighbor who cares, a clerk's quiet courtesy.
Grandpa's hands are gentle;
the poet soothes our soul.
Words of kindness create;
we are forgiven and made whole.
A carpenter's way with wood,
a mechanic's ability to fix,
a counselor's healing touch,
a homemaker's gift of food,
an athlete proving skill,
an artist painting wildlife,
a bright and alert mind used only to do God's will.
The gifts we've received from our Creator,
given in charity, given with love.

> That is why you, God,
> have chosen us and filled us with a glad heart.
>
> (Psalm 45:7)

30. *God's Love Stands*

> God is our shelter and strength,
> our help in times of trouble.
> We need not fear,
> even if the earth is shaken
> and the mountains fall into the sea.
>
> (Psalm 46:1–2)

There were times
when I could not keep my thought on you, O God,
or speak what I felt in my heart.
I was troubled, had so much to do,
and could not quit to be alone with you.
Then I listened to your words in music.
I played the song, again and again.
The melody washed over me;
the soothing words reached into my aching heart.

Though the mountains may fall
and the hills turn to dust,
yet the love of the Lord will stand,
as a shelter for all
who will call on His name.

(Daniel L. Schutte,
"Though the Mountains May Fall")

The music comforts me; your love is everlasting!
My heart is no longer troubled; I am not afraid.
Everything around me can crumble; I am secure.
God is my shelter; God is my strength.

    Sing the praise and the glory of God.
        (Schutte, "Though the Mountains May Fall")

31. *The Farmer*

    All people, clap your hands.
    Shout to God in joyful praise.
    God chose for us our land,
    the proud possession of a beloved people.
                          (Psalm 47:1–4)

Dear God, I love this land you placed in my care.
I love the smell of the soil, the promise of new life.
I can't wait to begin tilling the earth,
surrounded by wildlife, by signs of spring.
There's a freedom out here, working with creation.
Farming is probably the closest a person can get to
    God's work.
Often, my whole family brings lunch to the field.
They understand the value of my labor.
Sometimes, though, it's hard, God.
Today, I look back and can't see the disc and drill.
The air is filled with dust; we lack moisture.
With every fill of seed, I add my prayer for rain.
When we do get a crop, we need a just price.
I need to be treated fairly by those who buy my
    products.
My lender wants a mortgage on everything I have.
I need to work with people who have faith in the
    farmer.

You've given me so much, God,
and I'm truly thankful.
Help me always to show you that thanks by being
a good steward, a good spouse and parent,
a good person, a good farmer!
It's all I've ever wanted to be!

All the earth, revere your God.
Honor your Creator, all people!
By God's word, the world was created.

(Psalm 33:8–9)

32. *God, Our God*

Great is our God,
and to be highly praised!

(Psalm 48:1)

Almighty God,
creative love,
faithful guide,
secure shelter,
strong defender,
just ruler,
shepherd of the flock,
source of wisdom,
loving parent,
liberator of the enslaved,
healer,
refuge for the oppressed,
light to the world,
hope of all people.

This great God is our God,
now and forever.

(Psalm 48:14)

33. *Hunters*

All the animals of the forest,
all the birds of the heavens,
and all the creatures that live in the fields
are mine, says God.

(Psalm 50:10)

His letter said he wished
they could have walked our river bottoms
one more time before his dad's death.
This man,
like many of the guys who have hunted here,
works in an office during the week.
They come as much to walk and look and feel
as to take game.
They understand and value wildlife,
harvesting only what the law says
is necessary for correct balance.
They donate funds and time
to provide and preserve habitat.
We know that the land
and all that is on it
belong to our God.
We share the land on which we live with these men.
They help us with jobs on the ranch.
They are thankful
for the chance to hunt
and to be in the outdoors.
We are thankful
for the bountiful gift of the land.

The giving of thanks glorifies God.
I, the creator God, will surely save
all who honor me.

(Psalm 50:14–15)

34. I Know Myself

Be merciful to me, O God,
according to your kindness.
I am conscious of my faults;
my sins are before me.
You deserve a truthful heart
and a sincere spirit.

(Psalm 51:1–10)

God, we often place the blame for our troubles
somewhere else.
We recite our excuses:
"If they hadn't tried to cheat us";
"She said something first";
"If my husband only talked to me";
"The teacher isn't fair."
We allow ourselves to act
as victims of circumstances.
When I do that, God,
I don't have to look at myself.
If I make a mistake in judgment
or sin against your law,
I must examine and correct myself.
I cannot usually change the world around me,
but you have given me a free will,
a conscience.
With your grace,
I must convert myself,
transform myself,
according to your word.

Create a clean heart in me, O God,
and renew my spirit.

(Psalm 51:10)

35. A Handshake

God looks down from above
to see if there are any who are wise,
any who look for God.
There are none who do right;
all have turned away.

(Psalm 53:2–3)

Is the day of the handshake gone,
the day of trusting what a person says?
God, I'm disillusioned
about the honesty of people.
Appearances don't tell the story.
I feel real conflict
about the churchgoing, upstanding citizens.
Cheating starts at the top
and goes through all of society.
I used to think it was just the young,
but when older people get their back to the wall,
they do things they normally wouldn't do.
Dear God, I want to trust and help
the person across the desk from me.
Sometimes, people misrepresent conditions,
or they have no intention
of using the plans we work out together.
There are some who just satisfy the banker,
then do what they want!
The creditor should help them,
but they don't want to make changes
or do what may be necessary to help themselves.
O God, don't let those people get to me.
Remind me of all the good experiences:
the young people I helped through tough
        situations,

the many accomplishments made possible by our
    loans,
the good effect we have had on personal, business,
    and ag customers in our area.
Remind me of the people whose handshake
remains a symbol of truth and honesty.
Help me, God, always to be
the person my grandparents would be proud of,
a person of my word.

The words of good people are wise;
we say what is right.
The law of God is in our heart;
we are always fair and just.

(Psalm 37:30–31)

36. *Prayer of Sadness*

Listen to my prayer, O God,
don't hide from me.
Hear me and answer me;
I'm deeply troubled.
If it were an enemy against me,
I could endure it.
It isn't one who hates me
who does this to me.
It is my companion, my friend.

(Psalm 55:1–13)

He comes home, upset and hurt.
Another meeting didn't go well.
They say we must liquidate our ranch,
or they will foreclose on us.
We offer plans; they reject them.
Today is different from the other times they met.

He is devastated.
Today he was told,
"Don't take this personally; this is business."
The words were spoken by his friend.
What sadness when a friend turns away!
What pain pierces one's heart!

But I call upon God to save me.
God hears my voice and answers.

(Psalm 55:16–17)

37. A Broken Heartland

You have cast us off, God.
The land is broken apart,
and the people are distressed.
Heal our wounds, for we are shaken.

(Psalm 60:1–5)

God, it was a tough struggle.
I tried so hard to hold onto my business.
Some of my customers were overextended;
they just couldn't pay their accounts.
Others, fed up with low commodity prices, quit.
Some are gone through foreclosure, not by choice.
Finally, I had to hang it up too.
My business is gone; it's an empty building.
But the farms and ranches are still here.
The people leave; their children can't return,
and sometimes do not want to.
Their opportunity to farm is taken away.
They depart our area seeking a better chance.
Hardly ever does a new family move onto the land.
Usually, old neighbors snatch up parcels.

O God, you have given us the clearest skies,
abundant resources, caring people, little crime.
The value of education is seen
in the number of kids
who finish school
and go on for more.
Then, too many of them leave our state,
taking their youth and giftedness away from us.
Mindful God, who will live in this wonderful land?
Who will support our local businesses?
Who will bring children to our schools?
Who will sit in the pews of our churches?

Deliver your beloved people.
By your strength, we will be rescued.

(Psalm 60:12)

38. *Far from Home*

Hear, O God, my call;
listen to my prayer.
I am so far from home.
In despair, I cry to you!

(Psalm 61:1–2)

God, for all my life,
I lived on our farm.
Why have you allowed them
to take it from me?
My heart is breaking!
In the night, I could hear
owls hoot and coyotes howl.
Now, I hear
noisy teenagers and squealing tires.

I feel such sadness.
I awakened to
birds chirping outside my window.
Now I awaken to
doors slamming and cars starting.
I am so far from home!
Our country church was a family,
sharing joys and sorrows.
In this church, I'm one of so many;
does anyone care that I'm here?
I ache with loneliness.
Once, surrounded by God's creation,
I cooperated with nature.
Now, I labor indoors all day;
it's a job, a paycheck.
My heart is breaking.

O God, hear my cry of sadness.
Listen to my prayer.

> I take refuge in your love
> and find safety in your faithfulness.
> Heal my broken heart!

(Psalm 61:7)

39. *My Safe God*

> O God, my God!
> How I seek you.
> Like someone in a dry, weary, and parched land,
> my soul thirsts for you.

(Psalm 63:1)

Living God, I long for and want you as my God!
I take my children to your house;
I tell them of your greatness.
I ask you to bless our food
and to guard us in our sleep.
I thank you for your gifts and blessings
and ask you to show me your ways.
O God, do I really want to know your ways?
I am afraid to let you rule my life.
I want you to be my "safe" God,
to fit in your reserved place.
I want to be in my comfortable world
and not see the discomfort of others.
I want to hear music and friends' laughter
and not the cry of the distressed.
I want to feel good about what I earn
and forget that others do not have my gifts.

Your commandments hang on my bedroom wall,
but your law has no place in my work.
Why am I so uncomfortable, my God,
when I allow myself to drink deeply of you?

    As I lie in bed, I remember you.
    In the night, I meditate on you.
    I cling to you; your hand holds me.

(Psalm 63:6–8)

40. *The Rancher*

    It is fitting, O God, that we praise you.
    Blessed are they whom you choose,
    whom you bring to dwell in your sanctuary.

(Psalm 65:1–4)

Thank you, God, for these rolling hills,
the access to shelter for our cattle,
the wide-open spaces and fresh, clear air.
It's great to work and feel part of nature.
I love animals, both wild and tame.
I love this valley, the river, the trees.
There's nothing like a good herd of cattle.
Holy Friend, I most like being out on my horse,
feeling the power.
But I know I am steward, not master.
When the kids and their kids come home,
it's good to have their help and strength.
It's fun to watch grandkids enjoy the ranch.
Hopefully, gracious God, we can pass it on to them.
Life is good out here,
even though sometimes,
ranching's a tough way to make a living.

This nation lacks understanding
of our worth and our needs.
Know us and value us;
we contribute much.
Thank you, God, for the use of this land.
Help us always to treat it with care
and to appreciate it for the precious gift that it is.

> The pastures are filled with cattle,
> the hillsides joyful with life.
> The meadows are clothed with sheep,
> the valleys carpeted with wheat.
> All the earth shouts for joy!

(Psalm 65:12–13)

41. *A Time of Testing*

> You have tested us, O God.
> As silver is tested by fire,
> so have we been purified.
> You let us fall into a trap
> and placed heavy burdens on us.
> You allowed others to override us;
> we passed through fire and flood.
> Now, you have brought us comfort.

(Psalm 66:10–12)

It was not an easy time, God!
We could not have come through it
without knowing of your constant love.
Heavy burdens weighed us down.
We went through the difficulties.
You have not allowed us to fall.

We admitted our faults to you.
We cried to you for help,
and you answered us.
You tested us by fire;
we have been strengthened and purified for it.
Your power is great.
We sing praise to you for your great acts.
How wonderful are the things you do.
Our hearts are our offering to you.

Come and see the works of God.
Come and hear, all who fear God,
and I will tell you
what our God has done for us.

(Psalm 66:5–16)

42. *Rejoice! Be Glad!*

God, be gracious to us and bless us.
May your face shine upon us
so that your way can be known on the earth,
your saving power among all people.

(Psalm 67:1–2)

May the sower of good seed praise you, O God.
May all the peoples praise you.
May the shepherd of the flock sing for joy.
You guide every nation on earth.
May the steward of soil and water honor your glory.
May all people everywhere honor their God.
May the herders come before you in thanksgiving.
Let us sing for joy to God, who protects us.
May the gatherers of the harvest
be glad and rejoice.
What a rich bounty God's goodness provides.

You, our God, have blessed us.
May the people revere you, O God;
may all the people honor you!

(Psalm 67:7)

43. *Lifting Burdens*

Sing to God!
Extol God's holy name.
Prepare a way for the holy one.
Rejoice in the presence of God!

(Psalm 68:4)

O God, how often you use your people
to show your presence among us.
Our concern for other people
is lifted in prayer to you, God.
Our care and love of others
is shown in our charity.
We are patient,
giving time and making the extra effort.
We go the extra mile,
lightening the load of another.
Our words are kind and considerate,
reserving judgment for God.
We bear good fruit;
our gifts come from and belong to God.
Our homes are a safe place;
our hearts are a refuge.
We care for our families;
we belong to God's family.
We are makers of peace and justice,
lifting up your people.
We minister to those in pain
and counsel those in trouble.
We lift our voices in song,
giving praise and thanks to God.

> Blessed be God,
> who bears our burdens day after day.
> God is a god of victories, large and small.

(Psalm 68:19–20)

44. *My Refuge, My Rock*

In you, O God, I take refuge.
You are just; rescue and deliver me.
Incline your ear to me and save me.
Be my secure shelter, my safe rock.

(Psalm 71:1–3)

My God, rescue me from cruel men and women;
from their power, save me.
God, I trust in your justice.
Since my youth, I have always tried to trust you;
I have relied on you all my life.
I will praise you.
My life has been an example to many.
I act with compassion and give care to others.
I tell of your goodness.
My enemies slander me;
may those who hurt me be shamed and disgraced.
God of all power, hasten to help me.
I held a position of honor with them.
Now they act as if they don't know me.
I put my hope in you, my God.
You have taught me since I was young;
I tell of your wonderful deeds.
Now that I am old and my hair is gray,
O God, don't abandon me.
Be with me while I proclaim your glory
to all generations, old and young.
You have sent me troubles and suffering,
but you will restore my strength.

You will raise me to dignity;
You will comfort me again.
I will praise your faithfulness!

(Psalm 71:20–22)

45. *God Is Our Judge*

In the appointed time, I will judge
and I will judge with equity, says God.

(Psalm 75:2)

You have spoken to your people.
You tell us to obey your laws.
You teach us the way to go.
You instruct and advise us.
O God, I have searched the Scriptures,
and nowhere do I find that you ask us
to sit in judgment of one another.
And yet, we each judge.
We say who is good and who is evil,
declaring innocence or guilt.
We classify, categorize,
and hang labels on others.
Then we allow ourselves
to treat them accordingly.
By doing that,
we ease ourselves;
we ease our conscience.
We excuse and justify our own bad behavior.

Judgment does not come
from the east or from the west.
God alone is judge,
condemning some and lifting up others.

(Psalm 75:6–7)

46. *Bring Him Back*

I cry aloud, O God; you hear me.
I'm deeply troubled and lift my hands in prayer;
my tears flow, but I find no comfort.

(Psalm 77:1–2)

I lie awake all night long.
He is so close, so far.
Sometimes, he tosses and turns,
but we don't speak to each other.
I think of days long ago,
when we shared our hopes and fears.
I think of nights long ago,
when we found comfort in each other's arms.
But now, in his pain, in his fear, he rejects me;
he turns away.
We promised to share in good times and bad.
Does his promise no longer stand?
Has he stopped loving me?
I feel only his anger, not his love.
Why has he shut me out?
Why can't he trust his hurt to me?
The pain in my heart is deep, deep.
My whole being is troubled.
He is my love, my helpmate;
please, God, bring my husband back to me.

I meditate on the good you have done,
for your way is holy.
Help me, O God of miracles.

(Psalm 77:12–14)

47. The Ceremony

O God, they have invaded your land;
they have defiled your holy temple.
They have left the bodies of your people
to the birds and wild animals.
They have shed blood like water;
no one was left to care for the dead.

(Psalm 79:1–3)

The weekend of the State Finals Rodeo,
excitement and camaraderie filled all of us.
The opening on Sunday presented
four American Indian men from the Dakotas
who had been part of the movie
Dances with Wolves.
They rode in on horseback and in full dress.
The crowd respectfully watched and listened
during the opening ceremony.
Then, my nine-year-old grandniece and I
visited about the movie.
We talked about the way native people and culture
were shown in the movie.
I told her how native people
were presented in movies
when I was her age, many years ago.
Sometimes, we wish for children today
a return to what we call
"more basic values."
One thing I wish for is
more integrity in their history lessons—
more than we had.

Do not hold us guilty for the sins of the past;
have mercy and forgive us.
Then we, the people you shepherd,
will thank you and praise you forever.

(Psalm 79:8–13)

48. *Precious Creation*

O Shepherd of Israel, leader of the flock,
save your people.
You have given us sorrow to eat,
tears of great measure to drink.

(Psalm 80:1–5)

I have always believed, my God,
that your people are the most precious of all your
    creation.
Only your people have been created in your image
    and likeness.
And yet, in our struggles or our greed,
we harm one another.
We have more worth
than that over which we fight—
the land or the cattle that graze on it
or the crops that grow in the soil
or the minerals deep within
or the machinery used in production.
We are able to put a value on all of them.
Is it so hard, great God, for us to value one another?
We treat others badly
and then justify what we do by saying:
"It's my job."
"They can do it; so can I."
"If I wouldn't have, someone else would have."

The end we seek is usually honorable;
the means we use to achieve it is not always so.
We do not always treat one another with respect.
The end result does not justify the means we use.
O God, we wander from your teachings.
Reveal yourself, Holy Friend.
Bring us back to your ways.

> Turn us again to you, almighty God.
> Shine on us; in your mercy, save us.

(Psalm 80:7)

49. *The Advocates*

> God presides in the heavenly court,
> pronouncing judgment:
> "How long will you judge unjustly
> and show favor to the wicked?
> Defend the rights of the poor;
> be fair to the needy and helpless."

(Psalm 82:1–3)

They feel stripped of their rights,
believing the system is for the powerful.
For they have lost their power, O God;
a sense of helplessness overwhelms them.
They do not know how to defend themselves
against those with more knowledge and resources.
You, our God, instruct us
to help those less wealthy, less fortunate, less sure—
to make them aware of their rights, their value.
We use our abilities to lift up your people;
as their abilities are unveiled, hope increases.
As advocates, we educate, encourage, and empower.
We listen and guide, inviting their response.

We are instruments in your hands, O God,
for you alone are the source of our power.
Source of all wisdom, you are our teacher;
all knowledge is yours.
All goodness, righteousness, and truth
come from you.

> Arise, O God, and rule the world.
> All nations are your possession.

(Psalm 82:8)

50. Your Dwelling

> How I love your dwelling!
> How I long to be there.
> My whole being wants to be
> near to the living God.

(Psalm 84:1–2)

How I long, O God, to be in your house,
to be part of your church;
I am troubled and want to be near you.
When I approached a group after services,
they quit talking
and gave one another knowing glances and smiles.
They whisper behind our back,
saying we brought on our own troubles.
They hold themselves above us.
I am going through such a deep valley.
I pray constantly for strength;
fortify me with your strength.
Give me courage to go back to my church.
My money offering will be small,
but I present myself to you.

Let me sing again for joy
as I stand in my church,
as I stand in your presence, living God.

> God, you are our light and shield,
> blessing with grace and honor
> those who trust in you.

(Psalm 84:11)

51. Be Patient

> God will give us what we need,
> and our lands will yield a rich harvest.

(Psalm 85:12)

It's not easy, dear God, being an ag lender
in an area with such dry conditions.
We have to be patient
and make that extra effort to help our borrowers.
How many people do we have to lose
before we're willing to help them through it?
We've had to extend some loans,
but given time,
they'll work out of it.
We inform our borrowers of their situation;
there are no surprises if it doesn't work.
Some people come to us from other lenders.
They got in trouble from bad advice.
We need collateral and up-front honesty,
but we don't want to run their businesses.
Even though regulations are strict,
we do try to consider character and conditions.
Nothing is a bigger gift to me, God,
than to have people who came to us with problems
pay down or pay off their loans.

It's satisfying to know
that our help and patience
made a difference for them!
I'm not at all sure borrowers
know I care about them.
I do try.
Help me, courteous God.

> Kindness and faithfulness will meet;
> justice and peace will embrace.
> Our loyalty will spring up from the earth,
> and God's righteousness
> will look down from heaven.

(Psalm 85:10–11)

52. *Handmaid of God*

> Make glad the soul of your servant.
> I trust in you and pray to you.
> You, O God, are good and forgiving;
> rich in kindness to all who ask your help.
> I bow before you; you alone are God.
>
> (Psalm 86:4–10)

My mom was a loving woman, gentle of heart.
She enjoyed card games with Dad and their friends,
and preparing "banquets" for nieces and nephews.
She was their beloved Aunt Mary.
I wondered who or what
made my mom the person she was.
Life wasn't always easy.
She came to this country when she was fourteen
and worked long hours
to support her widowed mother.
Later, she worked with Dad in their store.
She longed for eight years
before their first child was born.
My mom's life, like everyone's,
had happy times and sad times.
Eventually, I realized
why she was able to love people so well.
She first loved the Creator of all people.
Her heart rested in God!
She taught me
by telling stories of people who served God.
Her favorite was Mary,
but many others came to life in her accounts.
She rarely criticized
and never gossiped,
but quickly saw goodness in others.

She obeyed God faithfully
and served with complete devotion,
offering full praise for God's goodness.
Even as a parent and grandparent myself,
I thank God each day for Mom,
beautiful handmaid of God.

> You are a compassionate, gracious God,
> patient, kind, and true.
> Turn to me and strengthen me;
> I serve you as my mother did.

> (Psalm 86:15–16)

53. *Fair Pay*

> Blessed are they
> who live in the light of your countenance.
> In your love, we are strong.

> (Psalm 89:15–17)

God, I need your strength;
I don't know what to do.
If I quit, who will take my place?
I believe in my skills as a lawyer,
I believe in the service I provide,
but I must get paid.
Is my work to save a farm worth less
than that of the person trying to take it away?
I recognize my client's limited ability to pay,
but it's frustrating not having that income.
It's scary knowing
that the lenders have more resources;
I know that their lawyers are paid monthly.
Should only the well-heeled have attorneys?
Will justice be served then, my God?

I want to be loyal to my clients
and available to others,
but I need fair and just pay too.

> Justice and righteousness
> are the foundation of your rule.
> Kindness and faithfulness
> are shown in all you do.

(Psalm 89:14)

54. *Show Your Colors*

> We will dwell in the shelter of God!
> The Almighty is our shield,
> keeping us safe from hidden dangers,
> protecting and defending us with faithfulness.
>
> (Psalm 91:1–2)

In spring's new life,
we take the kids for a ride.
They see a doe;
we know she has twins nearby.
She hides them so well that
even with binoculars,
we barely get a glimpse of them.
A noise startles a hatch of chicks;
we see movement in the brush.
Like the fawns, they blend into their surroundings.
We cannot tell
if they are pheasant, grouse, or partridge.
Only in fall will the young pheasant roosters
begin displaying their brilliant colors,
by which we can identify them.
We're a lot like the spring wildlife, creative God.
We want to blend into our surroundings.

We want to be part of the scenery;
we really don't want to be noticed.
But sometimes, God, you call us
to be bold, to show our colors,
to stand up, to act out.
You want others to recognize us as your own.
You want us to be identified as yours.
By our just and peaceful actions, God,
people will know we belong to you.
Fear and cowardice shake us, though,
and drive us into hiding!

> You need not fear any danger in the night
> or an arrow that flies in the day.
> God says, "I will save those who know me."

(Psalm 91:5–14)

55. *Where Is God?*

> God made our ears; can't God hear?
> God made our eyes; can't God see?
>
> (Psalm 94:9)

Farmers leave the land;
young people, our state.
Cities fight crime and problems of overcrowding.
God does not see.
A rich man illegally increases his wealth
and is set free;
a poor man steals
and is jailed.
Where is your justice, God?
People talk of poverty
and create programs to end it.
Poverty of spirit is a greater ill.
Who hears the cry of the poor?
Our words speak of points of light and heroes.
Our money manufactures bombs and bullets.
How much longer, God?
Injustice flourishes throughout the land.
The rich are richer,
and the numbers of the poor increase.
Will you hide yourself forever?
I ask, "Why do you allow suffering and sorrow?"
God searches my heart and asks, "Why do *you*
    allow it?"
God will not abandon the people.
A baby is born, good news to family and friends.
She will look to the world; what will she see?
God's work goes on.
God's love is eternal!

God will not abandon the people.
Judgment will again be just,
and all who are upright of heart will follow it.

(Psalm 94:14–15)

56. *Celebrate Life!*

Sing a new song unto God.
Sing to God, all the earth!

(Psalm 96:1)

Be glad, sky;
let your clouds dance and your sun glow.
Roar, sea,
and every creature in your great depths.
Exalt, O valleys;
bring forth your bountiful harvest.
Trees in the woods, shout for joy.
Hills, sing together before your Creator.
Rivers, clap your hands.
Flocks in the fields, dance in celebration.
Cattle on the grasslands, be filled.
Animals of the forest,
creatures that crawl,
all living things of the earth,
sing to God!

Sing to the Creator, all the earth.
Splendor and majesty surround you.

(Psalm 96:1–6)

57. The Law of the Land

God is our ruler!
Earth, be glad!
God the most high is above all the earth.

(Psalm 97:1–9)

While swathing hay, he sees the hawks overhead.
They hover, watching with keen eyes.
One swoops to the ground and back into the air—
swiftly, clutching a mouse in her talons.
A snake lies quietly in the grass.
A toad hops by.
In a flash,
the snake is fed for several days.
Nature's law pits the large against the small;
the swift against the slow;
the wily against the naive;
the powerful against the weak,
old, and young.
God gives us a different law,
a law based on love.
And yet, we watch big businesses and farms
swallow the smaller ones.
Those gifted with swift minds
close in on slower thinkers.
The powerful
devour the vulnerable.
O God, do we not know you as our just ruler?
Have we no knowledge of your laws?
How can we wish for goodness and peace on earth
when we lack it in our own heart and mind?

How disloyal their hearts are!
They do not know my laws.
They shall not enter the Promised Land,
the resting place.

(Psalm 95:10–11)

58. *Sing to God*

Sing a new song unto our God
for all the wonderful works.
Acclaim God, all the earth;
sing joyful songs of praise.

(Psalm 98:1–4)

She came to our church so long ago,
a quiet young bride.
She brought to us
a special gift for music.
Reserved and shy, she helped;
over time, she offered more.
She played lead guitar;
young people joined her.
She lifted her voice in song;
others gathered around.
With the children, she sings happy songs;
they celebrate a joyful God.
To our teens, she brings God's word;
it comes alive in her music.
In joy, she sings of God's faithful love
when two people wed.
In gentleness, she brings comfort and peace
to a grieving family.
On weekends, she leads us
in giving glory and praise.

She sings and plays for the goodness of God,
thanking God for all her gifts.
Blessed be this maker of music.

Make music to God!
Blow trumpets in joy and praise
to God, our God.

(Psalm 98:5–6)

59. The Law of God

Sing to God, all the earth!
Serve with gladness.
We belong to God, who made us.
Sing for joy to God, all the earth.

(Psalm 100:1–3)

We serve God
and live by God's law.
We rescue the poor
and lift the load off their back.
We give generously
to the needy and neglected.
We give homes to the homeless
and food to the hungry.
We support single parents
and provide companionship to their children.
We find jobs for the unemployed
and educate the unskilled.
We nurse sick bodies
and bring healing to wounded hearts.
We visit those imprisoned
and bring comfort to the dying.
We save people from oppression
and work for justice in all the land.

We give strength to the helpless
and have pity on the weak.

> Enter the gates with thanksgiving.
> Come into the courts
> giving praise and thanks to our good God.

(Psalm 100:4)

60. *Public Servant*

> My song is of kindness and justice.
> To you, O God, I will sing.
> My actions will be faultless
> if you give me your help.

(Psalm 101:1–2)

People see this as a public office.
Those of us who work here
hope we serve justly.
Many forces tug and pull on our staff;
so many demands, needs, and wants.
It's difficult to determine priorities.
We work to help people meet their needs,
to discern what is just and right,
to consider the interests of society.
Rural issues are important;
they affect the state and nation.
Often, we bring together
people with different views
so that they can listen to one another.
Hopefully, a just resolution emerges.
When people play it straight—
are honest and up-front—
looking for solutions,
we go to the wall for them.

If, occasionally, we sense dishonesty,
then we end up looking over our shoulder.
A waste of time and energy!
People think we can do more than we're able.
Some things are beyond our scope.
Then we inform, direct, and open doors.
We negotiate.
We don't always accomplish what we want.
The Psalms speak to me about
listening to God,
listening to the land,
and listening to the cry of the poor.
I listen and reassure people that we care.
Sometimes, merciful God, that gives them hope.
Be with me, God, for I am a servant.

> My song is of kindness and justice.
> To you, O God, I will sing.

(Psalm 101:1)

61. *Grieving for My Father*

> O God, I call to you for help.
> Do not turn away from me
> when I am so troubled.
> Hear my cry and answer quickly.

(Psalm 102:1–2)

O God, I miss him;
why did he have to die?
Did he feel pressure to save the farm
and keep it in the family?
We only encouraged him to do
what we thought he wanted.

Did those men have to say so unkindly
what a poor manager he was?
"Other guys are making it."
They made him feel worthless.
Was it just to break his spirit,
so he would quietly leave the land?
He didn't sleep well many nights.
Days, he worried while he worked.
The stress was too much for his heart;
it failed from the strain.
Dad, you were such a good man,
honest, fun,
neighborly, and hardworking.
I wish we could have
shown better the love you needed to see
and said the words you needed to hear.
Nothing—
not the land,
not anything—
was worth your dying.
Dad.
Dad.
O my God, I wish you were here!

Listen to my prayer, merciful God.

(Psalm 102:1)

62. First Americans

My spirit praises God,
who fills my life with good things.
My youth is renewed,
and I am strong like the eagle.

(Psalm 103:1–5)

I am a young American Indian.
My skin is brown, and my hair is black.
Brown is the color of Mother Earth.
Black is the color of the sky
before the life-giving rain falls.
My heritage is a precious treasure.
I feel no inferiority before white people.
White people have not taken our land;
they have only changed it.
We learn to live in this changed land,
to preserve and to protect it.
Our tools are no longer bow and arrow,
horse and lance.
Now, we work with heart and mind,
love of the land,
and hope for our children.
We will break any chains that still bind us.
Proud people, we will live free.

As high as the heavens are above the earth,
so great is the kindness and love of God
for those who are reverent and show honor.

(Psalm 103:11)

63. A Child Is Born

Praise God, my soul.
O my God, you are great.
You send forth your breath,
and all life is created.
You give hope to the earth.
May the glory of God last forever!
May you find joy in your creation.

(Psalm 104:1–31)

My first pregnancy—
an exciting time;
feeling our baby move within me,
selecting the proper food to nourish us both,
gathering clothes for her or him,
sewing a skirt for the bassinet,
choosing godparents.
All the preparation could not prepare me
for the wondrous joy
when our child was born!
I felt one with you, creating God.
When she was being knit in my womb,
you knew her.
She is your work;
she is wonderfully made.
Surely you have honored my husband and me;
you have allowed us to create with you.

> I will sing to God all my life.
> God is the source of all my joy.

> (Psalm 104:33–34)

64. *Doing Business*

> Give thanks for God's goodness
> and everlasting love.
> Blessed are they
> who are just and fair to others,
> who do what is right.

> (Psalm 106:1–3)

Holy Friend, I try to do what is right.
In the eighties, many of us paid for
the easy credit and high interest of the seventies.

It bothered me, merciful God,
when I had to go out to the country
to repossess machinery.
My suppliers did everything they could,
but sometimes, we had to foreclose.
I don't know of any time
we intentionally caused hardship.
We never picked up equipment
when it was needed.
Some folks were losing their place;
they had no need for machinery to run it.
Others knew there was no way
they could pay for what they had bought.
God, I try to treat people fairly,
the way I'd want to be treated.
We found out one thing through all of this:
we can't afford to be their bankers.
Some people who owe us don't seem to care;
others send a small amount monthly.
If everyone could send just a little!
People still buy used machinery.
Our repair work keeps us going.
Merciful God,
we are committed to our customers,
our town, our community.
Please, look with favor on your people;
show us your kindness.

 Let all of us see prosperity
 and feel the joy of your people,
 the joy of all who belong to you.

(Psalm 106:5)

65. *Decisions*

Growth in wisdom comes from reverence for
  God.
Sound judgment is given to all who obey God's
  law.

(Psalm 111:10)

Source of wisdom, I need sound judgment
and wisdom in my work.
Sometimes, my frustrations and questions
appear overwhelming.
The Psalms speak of your kindness and mercy,
my God.
How can I show those qualities
and still be fair?
Some of the farmers prove stable borrowers;
others struggle,
and a number are distressed.
Our borrowers vary in capabilities too.
Just and good God,
may I never vary
in the respect I give them.
In my business, balancing everyone's interests
confronts and worries me.
I care about our employees.
I answer to a board.
And, finally,
I'm responsible to the stockholders-borrowers.
I try to be consistent and creditable.
My goal is a win-win situation.
I come from a farm too;
I want to see farmers and ranchers succeed.
Ideally, we should mutually benefit.
I can't control the factors
that make someone successful.

I can only seek the truth and do my best.
Like farmers, I too am swept by emotions.
I can't judge only on them, though;
I need to be realistic.
Thank you, God, for the abilities you've given me.
Help me to use them to serve you and your people.

> Help me to be just and dependable.
> Guide my decisions with your truth.
>
> (Psalm 111:7)

66. *Servants in the Heartland*

> Blessed is the person
> who has reverence for God,
> obeying God's commands with joy.
> Blessed is the one
> who conducts a business honestly.
>
> (Psalm 112:1–5)

Dear God,
one of the joys of living in your heartland
is doing business with the people who are your
    servants.
They treat their customers with respect and
    courtesy.
They are generous to those in need,
not always knowing if they will be paid.
Their kindness never fails.
In trust, they leave parts outside their shop
and correct a receipt on a person's word.
They are caring, compassionate, and just.
They become a light for all good people.
They store up riches in heaven.

They are a light in the darkness for the upright,
for the merciful, kind, and just.
Their hearts are steadfast in God.

(Psalm 112:4–7)

67. *To You Alone*

Glory to you alone, O God.
Not to us, only to you.

(Psalm 115:1)

In our sowing and our reaping,
we give glory to God.
In our love and our discipline,
we give glory to God.
In our knowledge and our strength,
we give glory to God.
In our work and our rest,
we give glory to God.

In our music and our art,
we give glory to God.
In our writing and our reading,
we give glory to God.
In our learning and our teaching,
we give glory to God.
In our listening and our speaking,
we give glory to God.
In our seeing and our doing,
we give glory to God.
In our simple acts and our great deeds,
we give glory to God.
In our contrition and our praise,
we give glory to God.
In our petition and our thanksgiving,
we give glory to God.
In our living and our dying,
we give glory to God.

To God be the glory,
now and forever.

(Psalm 115:18)

68. *God Hears My Prayer*

I love God,
the one who hears my prayer and answers.
I call upon God all my days.
Fear and anxiety filled me.
Then I called upon God:
"O God, save your servant."

(Psalm 116:1–4)

Fear and anxiety plagued us;
We thought of nothing else.
We struggled hard;
we jumped the hoops,
but still we lost the farm.
Crushed,
I imagined that starting over again
would be impossible.
I'd lost trust in other people.
Even so, I kept believing in you, my God,
through the helplessness
and feelings of being worthless.
You would not let me be defeated.
In your mercy, you lifted me up;
you renewed my spirit and confidence.
You relieved my fears,
and you lifted my anxiety.
With you at my side, what should I fear?
Now we use our skills in new jobs;
we have a different life.
Sometimes, I cry and ache for home,
but you have guided us to a new one.
You, my savior, stop my tears.

> God saved me from death,
> keeping me from defeat, drying my tears.
> And so, I walk in the presence of God,
> in the land of the living.
> What can I do to repay you, my God,
> for all your kindness to me?

(Psalm 116:8–12)

69. *Truth and Justice*

You are a righteous God,
and your rules are just.
The heart of your law is truth;
your justice stands forever.

(Psalm 119:137–142)

We search in and depend on
the books of our law,
or loopholes and technicalities,
to defend truth and to do justice.
But our law
and our courts
and the politics of people
are too often about winning and losing.
Truth is not always an issue,
and justice not always the result.
So we can depend on another book of law.
If we live by God's law,
truth will shine,
and justice reign.

God, you have given us your laws
to obey faithfully.
I hope with all my heart
that I follow in your way.

(Psalm 119:4–5)

70. What Is My Worth?

I lift my eyes to the mountains;
from where will my help come?
My help will come from God,
the Creator of heaven and earth.

(Psalm 121:1–2)

How can I work all day
surrounded by the beauty of your creation
and feel of so little value?
Sometimes, I wonder if my value only comes
from the balance in my checkbook
or the clothes my children wear
or the machinery on the ranch.
On Sunday, our pastor told us
how we are created
in the image and likeness of God.
O God, why don't I quite believe him?
Why can't I know my worth?
I'm upset
by the control government agencies have
over this land, our livelihood.
I feel oppressed
by the large grain-trading companies
and livestock industry.
We are treated with contempt
by people who hardly understand agriculture.
O God, why can't others see our worth?

I lift up my eyes to you,
O God in heaven.
I depend on you, my God,
for your gracious mercy.

(Psalm 123:1–2)

71. *House of God*

> I was filled with joy when they said to me,
> "Let us go to the house of God."
>
> (Psalm 122:1)

He came to the little country church
to ask the pastor for food.
Services were starting,
so the pastor assured him
that he would share a meal with him afterward.
Then he invited the shabby old man
to come with him to the church.
The man was delighted.
People's eyes followed him
throughout the service.

They studied him
as he tried to join in song and prayer.
When it was time for the congregation
to wish peace to one another,
peace to all who enter in,
no one went close to the old man.
Then, finally, a child came,
touched his hand,
and said,
"God bless you real good."
O God, can we not give shelter in your house?
Even here, we quickly judge.
Even here, we withhold kindness.

> May there be peace inside your walls,
> and safety in your palaces.
> I say, "Peace be with you."
> God, our God, lives here.

(Psalm 122:7–9)

72. *On Our Side*

> What if God had not been on our side?
>
> (Psalm 124:1)

We are in his office,
seated across the desk from each other.
He is a righteous man
and believes that God is on his side.
I am your servant
and know that you, God, are with me.
In spite of that, we quarrel.
We argue over what is proper,
what is right.

Pushing a frayed thread
through a needle's tiny head
is easier than convincing him
to see my point of view.
In the Psalms, it appears clear
whose side God is on.
I want it to be that clear
to me today
in this room.
Surely we each can say,
"You, God, are for me
and embrace me as your own."
Are we so certain
that you embrace what we do?
Self-righteous,
self-serving,
can you embrace that?
Living God, let our concern be
that we are on your side,
not the other way around.
Grant us wisdom to understand your will
and courage to follow it.

> The law of God is perfect;
> it gives new strength.
> God's commands are trustworthy,
> giving wisdom and understanding
> to those who lack it.

(Psalm 19:7)

73. *Hostages*

When God brought back the captives,
it was like a dream.
We were filled with laughter;
we sang for joy!
God did great things for us;
we are glad.

(Psalm 126:1–3)

I had just dropped off my granddaughter
for an after-school class.
A radio voice announced
that hostages were freed
in a war-torn land far away.
The rush of emotions and tears took me by surprise.
I didn't realize how much I cared.
Maybe it was like other things
about which we feel helpless.
We pray;
we occasionally and sadly talk about it.
Usually, we tuck it away
in the recesses of our heart and mind.
Only when there is a resolution
do we understand the depths of our feelings.
My niece's card said simply:
"I am thankful
I can take the yellow ribbon off my car.
All our hostages are finally free!"
Now we wait to see the harvest of goodness
that can be reaped, with the grace of God,
from seeds sown in sorrow
and in violence.

Those who weep as they go forth
carrying the seed,
sing for joy as they return
bearing the harvest.

(Psalm 126:6)

74. Who Builds My House?

If God does not build the house,
the workers labor in vain.

(Psalm 127:1)

Is my life the house that is being built?
In the shifting winds of the world around me,
do I stand strong?
Is God my foundation, my rock?
When I make plans or set goals for my life,
does God guide me?
When walls in my life need to come down
and I must make changes to let in light,
is God the designer?
Does my house, my life,
have room for growth—
in faith, in love, in service?
Who is my architect?
If I tear apart what I do
from what I believe
and follow the guidelines set by others,
am I really allowing the Builder to do the work?

God, you are the builder.
As clay is in the hands of the potter,
so am I in your hands.

(Psalm 127; Jeremiah 18)

75. A Gift from God

Blessed are you who obey God
and live by the commands given you.
Your work will provide for your needs;
blessed and happy you shall be.
You and your spouse will be like a fruitful vine in
  your home,
your children like young olive trees around
  your table.

(Psalm 128:1–3)

O God, when I was young,
I prayed for your guidance in choosing a mate.
You sent him to me,
a quiet man with eyes that smile.
Little did he know how fruitful I hoped to be.
Many children came.
They enjoyed a full life on the ranch—
climbing hills, collecting rocks,
exploring caves, ice skating on the channel,
swimming in the river, fishing, riding horses,
building "houses" in their secret spots.
As they grew, so did their abilities
and their responsibilities
(farrowing, lambing, calving,
milking the family cow, rounding up cattle,
swathing hay, grinding feed)
and their endless activities
(4-H, FHA, FFA, CCD,
music, track, football,
basketball, horse shows, rodeos).
As activities increased,
our evening prayer became morning prayer.
On school days, as the bus came down the hill,
we were often gathered in prayer around the table.

On weekends during their teen years,
our night prayer was for their safe return
after driving gravel roads.
They are young adults now,
scattered because of jobs,
united because of love.
Our sons have their father's nature.
Our daughters hold him in highest esteem.
When they were home,
our house was full;
our hearts were full.
Now they return, some with mates and children.
Our house is overflowing;
our hearts too are filled to overflowing.

> Children are a gift from God,
> a blessing from above.

(Psalm 127:3)

76. *Trust in God*

> I have given up my pride, living God,
> and turned from my arrogance.

(Psalm 131:1)

I did things others noticed.
I said I did them for you
and for your people.
I was proud of what I did
and proud of what I said.
Sometimes, goodness turns into pride,
pride in one's goodness.
I am filled with arrogance, and not God.
There is no room for God
when I am filled with myself.

And still, I am so empty.
I turn and search for God.
In my honest moments,
my humble times,
I call out for God's help.
In great love, you come to me.
For you alone are God,
you alone.
Only in you can I place complete faith and trust.
Only in you can true contentment and peace be
found.

My soul is soothed and stilled,
like a child in its mother's arms.
My hope is in God, now and forever.

(Psalm 131:2–3)

77. A People in Disharmony

How pleasant it is
for God's people to live in harmony!

(Psalm 133:1)

You do not desire your people
to quarrel and fight among themselves.
But neighbors allow the fence between them
to become a wall.
They are jealous of others' success
and take delight when harm comes.
Lenders don't believe
the ranchers' count of their cattle
or the farmers' report of their crop yields.

Farmers mistrust
those who do their work on paper
instead of in the soil.
Townspeople resent
the programs
that benefit agriculture.
So bitterness invades our life,
plagues our relationships,
and eats at our heart.
Loving God, we become enemies in your sight.
How can we sing of our love for you
when we do not sing of our love for one another?

Anoint us, O God, in your righteousness.
Bless us with your wisdom and understanding.
Help us to live as a family in harmony!

(Psalm 133)

78. *Thank You!*

Give thanks to God for
everlasting love and kindness.

(Psalm 136:1)

You created me in your image and likeness.
Your love is everlasting.
You placed me in the loving arms
of a faith-filled family.
Your love is everlasting.
You surrounded me with relatives and friends
who guided me in your ways.
Your love is everlasting.
You gifted me with a free will to choose
good or evil, life or death.
Your love is everlasting.
You brought to me a spouse,
strong and tenderhearted.
Your love is everlasting.
You blessed us with children.
Your love is everlasting.
You touch my life constantly
with good and caring people
who seek to do your will.
Your love is everlasting.

Give thanks to God
for everlasting love and kindness.

(Psalm 136:1)

79. My Prayer

I sing praise to you, God.
When I pray, you answer me
and strengthen me.

(Psalm 138:1–3)

They do such terrible things.
Anger seethes inside me.
Have they no conscience?
Have they no feelings?
What kind of people are these?
They need help.
I pray to you, my God.
I lift them up in prayer.
Change their heart.
Give them some understanding.
Warm them with your love.
O God, help them.
God, you lift me up when I pray.
God, you change my heart.
God, you strengthen me.
God, you give me wisdom and understanding.
God, your faithful love swells within me.
Merciful God, I prayed for them,
but you changed me.

God, your work is eternal.
Complete your work in me.

(Psalm 138:8)

80. *You Know Me*

God, you have searched me
and you know everything about me.
You understand all my thoughts.
You see me when I am working or resting;
you know all my ways.

(Psalm 139:1–3)

How can it be that you understand me so well?
How can you know me?
I am only one of your children.
Wherever I go, in whatever I do,
you are present to me.
When I plant in the warm ground,
your sounds of springtime surround me.
When I cut hay in the heat of the summer,
your touch refreshes me.
When sadness weighs me down
through day after rainless day,
you comfort me.
In the darkness of short money and high costs,
you light my way.
You help me see the riches I do have.
Your goodness surrounds me
in the support of friends and family.
Your love is reflected
in the kindness shown by our children.
If I counted the kernels of grain in a field,
they would not be as many
as the good thoughts you have of me.

When I was being formed in my mother's womb,
you knew me.
You called me by name;
you chose me as your own.

(Isaiah 49:1)

81. Be Not Afraid

The God who created you says:
"Be not afraid, I have redeemed you.
When you pass through deep waters,
I will be with you;
you will not be overcome.
When you walk through fire,
you will not be consumed;
your troubles will not harm you."

(Isaiah 43:1–2)

O God, I am afraid!
The creditors are breathing down our neck.
The tension between my other half and me is
    unbearable.
My parents call asking for my help,
and our children take advantage of our distractions
    and walk us through fire.
Then a friend pats me and says,
"God never gives more than we can handle."
Get real! I scream inside.
This is more than I can handle.
I'm drowning in a sea of worry—
worry over money,
worry over my mate's anger,
worry over my parents' health,
worry over our kids' behavior.
O God, I need your help.

I cry aloud to God, begging for help.
I pour out my complaints
and tell all my troubles.
Hear my call, O God, help me.
I am sinking in despair.

(Psalm 142:1–6)

82. From Generation to Generation

I will exalt you, O God,
and thank you forever.
Great is God, and to be highly praised.
Each generation will tell the next
of your glorious works.

(Psalm 145:1–4)

Was it that long ago
that my mom and dad guided me in prayer?
Now, I pray with my children's children.
Our grandkids and I walk the ranch,
skip rocks on the river,
and watch deer feed in the corn.
We climb a hill and overlook the valley.
Together, we praise you, O God,
in the beauty of your creation.
At night, their warm, cuddly bodies
tumble onto the bed.
We thank you for the day.
The older children pray
for guidance and protection.
The smallest says, simply,
"God bless everyone in the whole wide world."

God is near to those who call with sincerity,
guarding those who love and praise the Creator.

(Psalm 145:18–20)

83. Listen to the Land

Sing in praise and thanksgiving to God,
who provides rain for the earth,
making grass grow on the hills,
satisfying with finest wheat.

(Psalm 147:7–14)

God of all the earth declares:
"Walk softly on the earth!
It is yours to use, not possess.
It belongs to your children's children.
Show care for the land.
Nurture it as I have nurtured you.
Sustain it, and it will sustain you.
You who live on the land be happy,
for you are chosen.
Be satisfied; I give you much.
Be good stewards of my creation.
Show reverence for this earth,
and you will give honor to your God."

God is pleased with those who show reverence,
with those who trust in God's constant love.

(Psalm 147:11)

84. Window to the World

Praise God from the heavens,
praise God from the earth.
Give praise, hills and mountains,
fruit trees and forests,
wild beasts and tame animals.

(Psalm 148:1–10)

I have my window to the world.
From our dining table,
I see the high cut bank,
the rolling hills,
the channel where the river once flowed.
On this winter day, little snow dots the brown hills.
Animals, tame or wild,
seem to have abandoned me.
Drought has left the channel bed bone-dry.
From my window,
I watched my children skating the channel
and sledding the steep hills.
But the seasons changed and the scenes changed.
For three springtimes,
we watched a bald eagle
nesting south of our house.
A fox had a den in the hillside.
Deer drank in the channel,
and a pack of coyotes wandered close to our home,
their howls spooking the night.
Grandchildren climbed the hills
and explored the caves their parents had probed.
Cattle grazed in the draws,
and horses roamed in a small pasture.
Barrels sat askew by the fence,
a reminder of hours of barrel-racing practice,
the sharp turns and close calls.
Wild turkeys paraded past,
and cottontails scurried, wary.
The seasons change;
the scenes change,
much like our life.
We have our times of drought and dormancy,
awakening and renewal.
Like the grass, we are cut back,
allowing new growth to take place.

Parts of our life end,
and there are new beginnings.
We grow through changes
in relationships,
in faith,
in our needs,
and in our giving.
Help us, dear God, to be more like nature,
willing—no, glad!—
to welcome the seasons in our life,
hoping for a glorious final resurrection.

Praise God, all peoples,
girls and boys,
old women and old men.
God's glory is greater
than all of earth and heaven.

(Psalm 148:11–13)

85. *Praise God!*

Praise to you, God, in your temple!
Praise your power in the heavens!
Praise you for your mighty works.
Praise your supreme greatness.

(Psalm 150:1–2)

Praise God in thunder and lightning.
Praise God in rushing rivers and gentle streams.
Praise God in clucking hens and grazing antelope.
Praise God in old women and strong young men.
Praise God in brilliant cardinals and calico kittens.
Praise God in shady maples and rows of carrots.
Praise God in rainbows and azure skies.
Praise God in newborn babies and tired workers.
Praise God in majestic mountains and rolling
    plains.
Praise God in frolicking lambs and beaver dams.
Praise God in waving grain and pasture flowers.
Praise God in generous farmers and hungry
    children.
Praise God in bawling calves and howling coyotes.
Praise God in the sunrise and at sunset.

Praise God in all the earth!

(Psalm 150:6)

"I use my Bible often in times of trouble or need, but I sometimes find the biblical readings hard to apply to my situation. With these psalms, I have just what I have been looking for. They have become my second Bible." **Marian Lefor**, rural life director, Diocese of Bismarck, ND

"To read *Psalms from the Heartland* is to experience the scriptural Psalms as contemporary writings and to be touched by the inner life of people of the land. These psalms will enrich the people of the heartland and others who wish to know them." **Rev. Ronald Gladen**, executive assistant to the bishop, Western North Dakota Synod, Evangelical Lutheran Church in America

These eighty-five psalms from the heartland, by Judy Hoff, express a full range of experiences of life in rural America. Some psalms thank and praise God for bountiful crops, comforting relationships, and the beauty of creation. Others lament the loss

of a farm or business, the precariousness of the weather, and the sadness of grown children moving away. Even though written about life in the Dakotas, the psalms will touch readers from any place.